Percussion Instruments

Music Makers

THE CHILD'S WORLD®, INC.

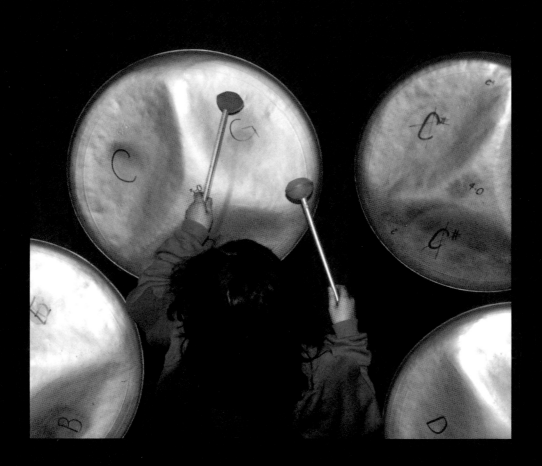

Percussion Instruments

Kayla Grace

THE CHILD'S WORLD®, INC.

On the cover: This girl is learning to play the timpani.

Published in the United States of America by The Child's World®, Inc.
PO Box 326
Chanhassen, MN 55317-0326
800-599-READ
www.childsworld.com

Product Manager Mary Berendes
Editor Katherine Stevenson, Ph.D.

Library of Congress Cataloging-in-Publication Data
Grace, Kayla.
Percussion instruments / By Kayla Grace.
       p. cm.
ISBN 1-56766-986-7 (lib. bdg. : alk. paper)
1. Percussion instruments—Juvenile literature.
[1. Percussion instruments.]   I. Title.
ML1030 .G73 2002
786.8—dc21
                                    2001005979

Photo Credits
© Bob Winsett/CORBIS: 19
© 2003 Bruno De Hogues/Stone: 9
© CORBIS: all images on page 23
© Corbis Stock Market/George Shelley, 2003: 15
© Jennie Woodcock, Reflections Photo/CORBIS: 20
© Paul A. Souders/CORBIS: 16
© 2003 Paul Harris/Stone: 13
© Steve Meltzer/WestStock: cover, 2
© Ted Spiegel/CORBIS: 6
© 2003 Terry Vine/Stone: 10

Table of Contents

6

Music is everywhere. We hear it on the radio, in the movies, at sporting events, and even during our favorite cartoons! There are many different kinds of music, too. But all music has one thing in common, no matter whether it is rock, country, classical, or rap. It has a beat, or **rhythm**.

Most of the instruments that provide music's rhythm are called percussion instruments. Percussion instruments make sounds when you hit them.

How Old Are Percussion Instruments?

Percussion instruments have been around for thousands of years. In fact, they are the oldest type of instruments in the world. Long ago, early humans made rattles, scrapers, and drums—often from animal skins and bones!

Percussion instruments have played important roles throughout history. They have been used in religious ceremonies. They have been used to send messages over long distances. They have even been used to send coded instructions to soldiers during wartime.

These Burundi drummers are playing on handmade drums. ➔

Are There Different Kinds of Percussion Instruments?

There are many different kinds of percussion instruments. All of them fall within two main groups. Instruments in the first group can produce only one note, or **pitch**. Examples of this type are snare drums, triangles, tambourines, and cymbals. Instruments of the second type can produce a wide range of pitches. Examples of this type are xylophones, steel drums, and chimes.

← This girl is playing a tambourine in Argentina.

What Do Percussion Instruments Look Like?

Percussion instruments come in many different shapes and sizes. Some, such as cymbals and triangles, are made of metal that is bent or flattened into different shapes. Others, such as maracas, are made of wood and look like rattles. Still others, such as chimes and xylophones, have parts of many sizes, made of metal or wood. The different-sized parts produce different notes when you hit them.

Here a Russian man plays a drum covered with an animal skin. ➜

How Do Drums Make Sounds?

Of all the percussion instruments, the most famous is the drum. Most drums are made by stretching a thin skin, or **membrane**, over a round frame of wood or metal. When you hit the skin, it makes a sound. The frame keeps the skin tight. It also acts as a **resonator** to make the sound louder—like cupping your hands around your mouth when you yell. The most common types of drums are the snare drum, the bass drum, and the kettle drum.

This father is teaching his son how to play a bongo. ➡

How Do You Play a Percussion Instrument?

Percussion instruments make noise only when you hit them. To play some percussion instruments, you hit them with your hand. To play others, you hit them with a hammer or **mallet**. Some hammers are simply pieces of wood. Wooden drumsticks are very simple hammers. Other hammers or mallets are padded to create different sounds.

← These men are playing glockenspiels at a festival on Panay Island.

What Do Percussion Instruments Sound Like?

Many percussion instruments can make only one sound. The bass drum produces a deep BOOM-BOOM. Cymbals make a metallic CRASH, and snare drums produce a sharp RAT-A-TAT-TAT. These instruments are used to help keep the beat. Sometimes they are used for a special sound. Other percussion instruments however, can play many different notes. Some can play a series of notes that go up or down to form a **scale**.

This person is playing a snare drum with drumsticks. →

How Do Percussion Instruments Make Different Sounds?

Many things determine the sound a percussion instrument makes. How hard you hit the instrument makes a difference. So does the type of hammer you use. Hitting a drum with a wooden drumstick produces a sharp, clear sound. Hitting it with a padded stick makes a quieter sound.

← This girl is learning to play bars like those on a xylophone.

On some drums, such as the kettle drum, you can change the drum's sound by tightening the skin. The tighter the skin, the higher the sound. On percussion instruments with different-sized parts, such as chimes and xylophones, the bigger parts make lower sounds. The smaller parts make higher sounds.

No matter how it is produced, the sound of the percussion instrument is one of the most important sounds in all of music!

Other Percussion Instruments

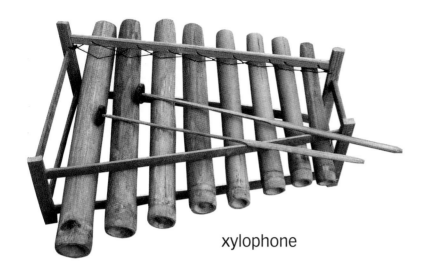
xylophone

triangle

guiro

castanets

sleigh bells

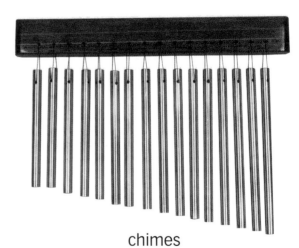
chimes

shaker

vibroslap

claves

23

Glossary

mallet (MAL-let)
A mallet is a hammer or stick used to hit many types of percussion instruments. Some mallets are padded to make a softer sound.

membrane (MEM-brane)
On drums, a membrane is a thin piece of calfskin or plastic stretched across the top. The membrane produces a sound when you hit it.

pitch (PITCH)
In music, pitch is how high or low a note sounds. Some percussion instruments can produce only one pitch, while others can produce more.

resonator (REZ-uh-nay-ter)
On musical instruments, the resonator is the part of the instrument that makes the sound louder. The body of a drum acts as a resonator.

rhythm (RITH-um)
In music, rhythm is a regular, repeating set of sounds or beats. Percussion instruments are often used to provide rhythm.

scale (SKALE)
In music, a scale is a series of notes that change in pitch one step at a time. Some percussion instruments can produce notes that form a scale.

Index